The Silver Pen

Sound and Silence

Jan Voth Dubbs

Jan Dubbs

Ready Writer

authorHOUSE®

AuthorHouse™
1663 Liberty Drive
Bloomington, IN 47403
www.authorhouse.com
Phone: 1 (800) 839-8640

© 2018 Jan Voth Dubbs. All rights reserved.

No part of this book may be reproduced, stored in a retrieval system, or transmitted by any means without the written permission of the author.

Published by AuthorHouse   07/17/2018

ISBN: 978-1-5462-5130-9 (sc)
ISBN: 978-1-5462-5128-6 (hc)
ISBN: 978-1-5462-5129-3 (e)

Library of Congress Control Number: 2018908228

Print information available on the last page.

Any people depicted in stock imagery provided by Getty Images are models, and such images are being used for illustrative purposes only.
Certain stock imagery © Getty Images.

This book is printed on acid-free paper.

Because of the dynamic nature of the Internet, any web addresses or links contained in this book may have changed since publication and may no longer be valid. The views expressed in this work are solely those of the author and do not necessarily reflect the views of the publisher, and the publisher hereby disclaims any responsibility for them.

Scriptures were taken from The New American Standards copyright 1960, 1962, 1963, 1968, 1971, 1972, 1973, 1975, 1977, 1995 by The Lockman Foundation

Holy Bible, New International Version®, NIV® Copyright ©1973, 1978, 1984, 2011 by Biblica, Inc.® Used by permission. All rights reserved worldwide.

DEDICATION

The words in "Sound & Silence" are dedicated to the glory of Lord Jesus. They are to Him, for Him and inspired by Him.

ACKNOWLEDGMENTS

Thank you and blessings, especially to my friend Gale Schadewald for graphic design; Emma LeVane for support and typing, Morgan Albertson, Nina, Donna Kusik, Richard Valdez, Jacque Valdez, for editing and encouragement and to my family: Beth, Tim, Emma, and Dan for putting up with me.

Contents

Introduction viii

Chapter 1 Words 1

Chapter 2 Sound and Silence 8

Chapter 3 God's Creatures 14

Chapter 4 Struggles 28

Chapter 5 Depths of Despair 38

Chapter 6 Lift Up Your Eyes 58

Chapter 7 Jesus our Messiah 70

Chapter 8 Peace and The Exchanged Life 82

The Silver Pen

Introduction

The Lord calls me His Ready Writer as scripture speaks of in Psalms 45:1.

"My heart overflows with a good theme as I address my verses to the King. My tongue is the pen of a ready writer."

He also tells me He has given me a silver pen. So with that pen I began to be that writer of these poetic works in worship and love and at times in the depths of depression, grasping towards His wonderful hand to always lift me up.

I love to be surprised by a truth that has lain quietly for several lines and then leaps up and bites me, the unsuspecting reader. Therefore, I have attempted to use a word not usually found with another in the same sentence and bring newness or unexpectancy to an otherwise simple line. It is a "suddenly" when the God of the Universe crashes into your tiny existence.

Jesus Christ is "The Word," which certainly gives more honor and glory to the simple word, "Word".

"In the beginning was the Word, and the Word was with God and the Word was God." John 1:1

"And He is clothed with a robe dipped in blood, and His name is called The Word of God." Revelation 19:13

Words are significant in our life, just as the Word of God was from the beginning of everything.

I love playing with words. Some leave a physical feeling in your mouth. The word for butterfly in German is schmetterling, while in Spanish it is a softer, sweeter sound, mariposa. I try to foresee if the poem will be read aloud or pondered over while resting in a comfy chair.

The depth within one word can contain many levels of meaning. The Lord says "choose only the word stones I tell you and when to hurl them onto the page." Then the words He gives me can have the power of boulders or the tenderness of feathers. I may even hurl them at a giant of unbelief.

Chapter 1

Words

As a writer, I look at "words" like a sculptor views clay. However, I do not change the actual word itself, but its surroundings.

They can pour forth like oil that is meant to anoint the reader and fill in cracks left by the hurt of loneliness. Some words even struggle into places where nothing else has ventured to go.

The Word of the Lord pours into my heart as if I am filling my silver pen with ink of gold.

Words, at times can be treasures like those hiding in Grandma's button box. "Oh, this one is perfect."

Words can be tasty like nuts when released from protective shells and made into treats that feel powerful as they roll off the tongue.

However, I know that words sent as shrapnel can explode into a living soul, as when a word is sharp as a dagger that drives deep within one, meant to hurt.

Words can be like living water, which washes off aching bodies and refreshes the dying.

His words press into my cheek and sleep rolls down my eyelids. Leftover energy seeps out through my dreams, where I run in fields of glory, never to tire.

Word Wrestler

I want to scatter my words across this page as a gardener who is slinging seeds into rich soil beneath his feet; to perceive new ways for transplanting seedlings of words, not just new ideas. I want to discover one word following another, that have never met each other before in a sentence.

The mind gets used to seeing thoughts presented in expected descriptions which put the brain to sleep before the period at the end of the sentence. Grab that thought, wrestle it to the page, and release it to stand surrounded by new adjectives and unexpected structures.

What is that slide doing in the middle of the highway? It's perhaps a new way to slip into another dimension or expand the purpose of the slide by simply taking an innocent by standing word and explode the reader into another membrane of existence as the Kingdom of God.

As in Hebrews 1:3, the writer says, "He (Christ) upholds all things by the word of His power." No capital for "word" here because He didn't say "by the power of His Word" which of course He could have. My mind stops to consider the difference before I jump into a moat of thought eating alligators.

Gone Fishing

LORD, would You go fishing with me today? I've tried without You before and I didn't get any worthwhile bites. You knew Peter wasn't getting even a nibble all night and You guided him to the "other side" of the boat which left his net so full of fish that he could hardly pull them into His boat. Jesus said to them, "Come and have breakfast."

Catching words for this page is like grabbing fish from the water. I must wait patiently until I hear the LORD say, "Catch this one." "Cast your pen on the other side of the boat." "Not that word, this one. It is so much more delicious." What a magnificent breakfast You have provided LORD.

Sometimes Yeshua even lets me catch an entire school of words. May they nourish others who are hungry for His Word.

Daddy, Open Its Door

Dust is well-known to the walls and seems to continually seep up between the wooden floor slats. Its rising is captured by the warm streams of light and clings to grubby windows. Standing in the middle of this memory of dingy deterioration, one wonders where the farmers are now, who were dressed either for a burial or a well-deserved Sabbath.

The only colors in this memory are her red curls surrounding speckled cheeks and bright pink hair clips. She reaches into a bowl of peanuts, hiding in their shells all the while gentle laughs and stories of the week on their tractors and combines are shared. Their struggles with withered crops are heavy on their minds, yet she is most interested in the small brown peanut that her hand had retrieved; turning it over and carefully examining it for a way to understand its bumps and hard exterior. She looks to the one whom she believed knew everything, "Daddy, open its door."

Jesus takes her hand today (the one that held the shell that was closed to her) and says "The peanut holds the mysteries of life. Lift up your eyes and look. The hand that cracked the peanut for you was your earthly Papa. Today your Heavenly Abba shows you mysteries and how to reveal them to others. Your Daddy pressed and released their magnificent and delicious interior. I have pressed you hard and am releasing words for others to read and feast on. Otherwise, they would simply lie in the bowl and gather dust.

Chapter 2

Sound and Silence

"Be still and know that I am God" Psalm 46:10 NIV

As a child I wondered how my deaf and mute grandparents perceived silence or how God communicated with them. I knew from very young childhood they could show me more love than anyone who could speak aloud; even though I hadn't yet learned their sign language.

I now watch faces and eyes when I communicate with others along with hearing their words. We need both sound and silence. I need it to survive.

Sound seems to sweep energy out of my soul; even delicate decibels dance across my eardrums, drawing attention and quickly change to a nearby timbre before I can draw meaning from it.

How can the Holy Spirit possibly be heard over such a cacophony of unholy sounds? I thirst for His still small voice, and pray for the dissonance of life to cease for a brief moment.

> Silence Slides in
> Stillness begins
> I feel lulled by the softness of your lullaby. Your quiet words have no sound, yet speak thunderously into my heart.
> "I love you."

Silence Behind the Torn Veil

"I will lead her into solitude and there I will speak to her heart." Hosea 2:14 NIV

"Be silent all flesh before the Lord." Zechariah 2:13

Silence settles into the cracks left in my soul by verbal shrapnel of countless voices where all my energy leaked out. Quietness soothes and begins the urgent restoration from a now distant dissonance which caused me to become deaf to another's needs. My jagged nerves repel all who surround me. "Go away and keep off my boundaries."

Bathing in a laver of silence, there seems to be a lathering up of the blaring blemishes caused by life outside this temple. Droppings of life which have splattered into my mind begin to slide off and I sink deeper into the fragrant waters of the Word.

Was it quiet behind the pristine veil? Could one hear the tinkling bells on the high priest's robe which swayed as he carefully moved to bring his sacrifice without making a single error? Were other priests listening from the outer court, and could they also hear the audible voice of God? It is quiet now behind my torn veil. I know the outer court (world) can cover up the voice of God so I must protect my time spent before the altar with Jesus. Peace gently falls on rough bundles of nerves and is reflected on the sea of glass.

Muffled sounds mystify my memories of the world's sharp edges. Silence does not change what lies outside. However, it has washed clean the memory of clatter and piercing words. I have been changed within the veil as Jonah was within his fish-shaped prayer closet. My refreshed mind, will, and emotions are once again able to sense another's pain and I am equipped to wash their feet in love. Thank you, Lord for my shower of silence and for letting it rain down into my heart.

"But the Lord is in His Holy Temple: let all the earth be silent before Him." Habakkuk 2:20 NIV

Soul Song Duet

Silence slides in and I am lulled by your voice. The stars above us agree with the wonder of our moments together.

My soul has been damaged by verbal attacks from one who wants to destroy who I am.

Quiet love dives into the deep cracks in my soul, soothing the jagged nerves, ready to ring an alarm: "Intruder".

Gentle words and quietness quenches my thirst for peace. My desire for a soul song duet poised like snow piling up on a branch.

    Then suddenly, silently it
        crashes down, changing the moment.
We lay quietly in each other's arms. He whispers poetic notice of beauty, which soaks and drenches me as kisses cover the disappearing cracks.

"My sheep hear My voice, and I know them, and they follow Me."
John 10:27

The Shepherd's Voice

Oh quiet my soul. Turn down the noise of daily life: other voices, my own voice, TV, cell phones, computers, traffic, music, air conditioning, lawn mowers, dishwashers, washing machines, machines, and more machines.

I wonder if my deaf-mute grandparents had an easier time of "hearing" the LORD than their "non-handicapped" children and grandchildren.

I have a monumental task when I try to turn off the noise in my mind and ears. It's those thoughts (mind noise) that keep popping up that distract me from prayer. Did Jonah think about the mundane in his watery prayer room, or just say, "Forgive me, LORD. Help me out of here!"

I strain to hear His voice, to filter out all of the extraneous sounds. In silence, I hear my heart beating. Why is it so hard to focus my ears on the shepherd's voice, which He says all His sheep know?

Chapter 3

God's Creatures

Life lessons come from every nook and cranny of my existence. When I spot one, it is like finding a treasure that God has lovingly placed there just for me to find. Even when it is a hard lesson, one that has caused pain or tears; I know that love is leaving me a note.

In this chapter, I share with you, examples of a few treasures I have found through God's creatures. I love God's messages to me, written in fur and feathers.

Blue Heron Moments

Blue Heron, oh so silent on your stilts as you stand and wait for that little fish snack to swim by. I am awed by those giant wings which quickly lift your slender body beyond my earthbound vision.

Just in time this wave of silence misses the grating sounds of "graaaakle". The grackles and herons are both birds, yet so different, like the difference between a diamond and a piece of coal. Both are birds just as both are carbon.

How often am I like the grackle bird, Lord? Irritating and annoying, I do have grackle moments. Thank you for my Blue Heron times when quiet beauty patiently waits for your tasty words to swim by. I quickly grab them as they make thunderous sounds inside my soul.

Follow the Lion

I see footprints leading me up the mountain. I keep following them as I realize He is letting me catch up with Him. Now He pauses to drink from the river and looks back at me. I know this lion could kill me.

He doesn't, and He moves on. I plead with Him to show me the top of His mountain. "Show me your land." I long to be there with You in your Land of Judah."

I follow the Lion of Judah into His Kingdom.

Spring Cleaning

Prairie dogs are cleaning house: throwing dirt, slinging out every speck of dirt from their mansion. Now they suddenly stand at attention like a guard; ready to race back inside for more attention to chores.

The Stillness of My Soul

"He makes me lie down in green pastures; He leads me beside quiet waters." Psalms 23:2

The camouflage of stillness is equivalent to something hiding in plain sight, like a rabbit when he sits among the rocks, not moving a whisker or an eyelid. It's the stillness that allows the deception. I wonder if its little heart is beating very fast or even at all. I see the life deep within that blackness, ready to pounce away to safety when a threat appears. How precarious the existence of this lop-eared creature. He reminds me of the life saving feature of complete stillness, just waiting, rather than bounding into trouble and jumping into another's space or mouth.

I remember looking into a microscope at the apparently meaningless movement of particles which seemed to move by bumping into each other and on and on. I also do meaningless things, just bumping into life, when I could be absolutely still and experience His magnificent presence which leads to bringing Him glory.

Quietness now sits on my soul as snow poised on branches, piling up then suddenly, silently crashing down; changing the moment. It is thunderously quiet; the stillness of a solitary soul.

"Surely I have composed and quieted my soul; like a weaned child rests against his mother; my soul is like a weaned child within me." Psalms 131:2

The Cricket Knows Seasons

The cricket knows the season of its end is near as days shorten and their chirping slows. If the cricket was created to know its cycle is complete and its end is near; why can't I know, too?

LORD, show me more as the seasons of fall come once again and the blowing of the Trumpet (Rosh Hashanah) approaches. It calls us into a time of awe and on to deep repentance (Yom Kippur) because of the emptiness of my vineyards.

Now I, too, notice the signs of the darkening days; being displayed before me in mighty reports. May my chirp increase rather than decrease. Let my voice be heard loudly as the season is changing. Come quickly and tabernacle with Him.

Blow a Trumpet in Zion

"Blow a trumpet in Zion, consecrate a fast, proclaim a solemn assembly." Joel 2:15

It's time. The geese left at the first crunches of winter to form their precision lines toward the South as their honking brings forth notice of the solemn assembly for the Day of Judgment.

High Holy Days and Days of Awe lead to repentance. Now sitting in a sukkah*, watching the geese arrive, we acknowledge what else is to come. He who was born in a sukkah will sit on a throne.

Prophetic Vision:
Six geese pass by and I wonder where the seventh is. Plumes of smoke rise up over a number of cities; the dead multiply. Waves of heat rise from the center one and continues for years. Trumpeters announce the meaning of the seventh. One city will die, bringing down a great and mighty nation.
It is time to blow a trumpet in Zion.

*sukkah- a temporary structure built to celebrate the Feast of Tabernacles and to commemorate the exodus of the Israelites from Egypt

Chapter 4

Struggles

"Do not be anxious about anything, but in everything by prayer and petition, with thanksgiving, present your requests to God. And the peace of God, which transcends all understanding, will guard your hearts and your minds in Christ Jesus." Philippians 4:6

"Consider it pure joy, my brothers, whenever you face trials of many kinds, because you know that the testing of your faith develops perseverance." James 1:2-3

Find His presence among chaos and disorder. He is always there with us. When you ask, "Why would God be here in this mess?" It is because that is where we are.

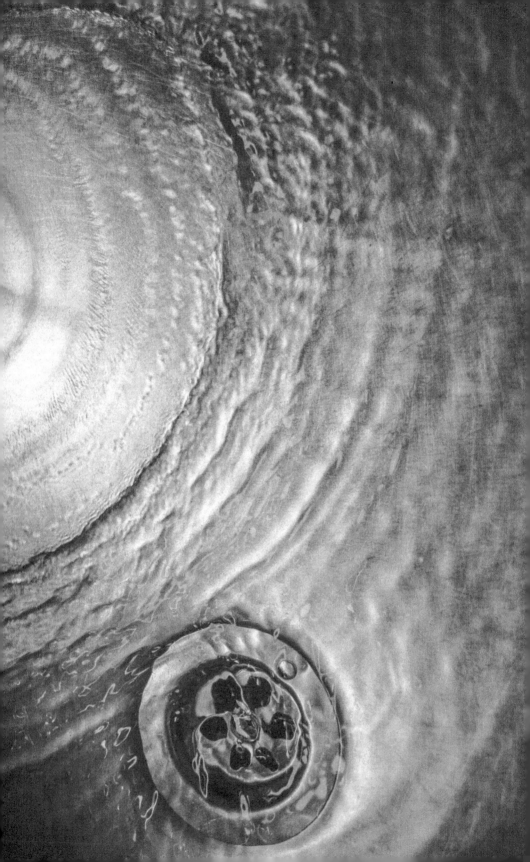

Cleansing of the Day

City life is lifted off of my face and I ease into such a tiny pool of peace. Layers float onto buoyant bubbles and waves of warm hope soak off tired troubles that have tied up muscles thought to be missing in action.

This earthly traveler is no longer weighted down with worry, or wearing garments of struggle that have been patched with anger and disappointment.

Clinging to the sides of this porcelain lays layers of the day ringing around as though announcing the Jurassic Period.

There is such pleasure in watching this day's dissolved remnants swirl around towards the drain. Do the early hours go down first or the most ugly and difficult moments?

Wrinkled fingers massage nearby muscles which still hold memories of the day which are now urged into a cocoon of sleep.

Exhaustion

My shoulders sag into my pillow as if rusty and needing oil. They are creaking with use or misuse; they whine for rest. But what have they done all day? They just held up the world which the LORD did not ask of them.

God doesn't appreciate what He doesn't initiate.

I look forward to exhaustion for your glory and it will feel good to be alive for Him.

Judge Not by What You See

Be not deceived by the outer structure. It may disguise wondrous treasures within.

> That blind man may see in the spirit and beyond the stars.

> The deaf may hear the LORD's voice more gloriously than the hearing can perceive.

> The scarred face may have a smooth and soft spirit that others long to touch.

"And like one from whom men hide their faces, he was despised, and we esteemed him not." Isaiah 53:3 NIV

Of No Stately Form

Jacob, Abraham's grandson, chose Rachel over her sister Leah because she was beautiful.

"And Leah's eyes were weak, but Rachel was beautiful of form and face. " Genesis 29:17

However, the Lion of the Tribe of Judah burst forth from this weak eyed, less beautiful tabernacle.

"Or do you not know that your body is a temple of the Holy Spirit who is in you, whom you have from God, and that you are not your own." I Corinthians 6:19

This Leah shaped tent had an outer structure of no stately form or majesty that we might stop and gaze upon her.

"He (Christ) has no stately form or majesty that we should look upon Him, nor appearance that we should be attracted to Him." Isaiah 53: 2

My own tent is rumpled and tattered, having been patched and repaired a few times. The desert tabernacle, whose outer linen curtain was sturdy and well-worn after years of wandering, stood strong to surround the presence of God. The LORD does not need a beautiful structure through which to bring His glory, just a humble vessel that can follow the cloud and pillar of fire.

Chapter 5

Depths of Despair

God hasn't told us there won't be times of despair, but how to deal with it.

Jesus tells us, "These things I have spoken to you, so that in Me, you may have peace. In this world, you will have tribulation, but take courage, I have overcometh the world." John 16:33

Dear Reader,
This is to share with you, Jesus knows. He has been there. The poems in this chapter reflect that I too have been at the bottom of the pit. I know that He overcame the entire world and therein lies why we should take courage.

The Cave

"The cords of death encompassed me, and the torrents of ungodliness terrified me. The cords of Sheol surrounded me; the snares of death confronted me." Psalms 18:4-5

I've slipped out of sanity and into a place of nothingness where I hear "Let go. Just let go." How far can I go? Sliding farther into the cave, it seems to welcome me back.

Somewhere in this cavern of pervasive sadness, thoughts penetrate into an explosion of sounds, bouncing off the walls that come alive with "You belong here, you belong here, you belong here."

Cave walls lean into ever increasing darkness. How can one ever get out? Do I ever want to? My cheek rests on the cold, still, vertical slab and I agree to stay.

A shiver shakes my soul and distorts my vision as moisture finds furrows previously plowed down my cheeks into pools of self pity. I hear it again, just a whisper: "Let go. Let go."

That is not my voice. It's pretending to belong and to be holding the umbilical cord of my life. God Help Me!

"And He sent out His arrows and scattered them, and lightning flashes in abundance, and routed them. He sent from on high, He took me, He drew me out of many waters. He delivered me from my strong enemy." Psalms 18: 14, 16, 17

Mummy Case of Despair

"Turn to me and be gracious to me,
For I am lonely and afflicted.
The troubles of my heart are enlarged;
Bring me out of my distress." Psalms 25:16-17

No! I don't want to be a flower pressed between pages, a dried memory where its life is gone and all fragrance squashed into oblivion. Don't put me in your scrapbook with glue, then just close the book and put me on the shelf.

But where am I now? Am I on a shelf glued into a book? It does feel like a container with no exit and the walls begin to move toward me. My thoughts become disconnected and crumble into the background.

Where do I end and where does the enclosure begin? I'm just in another box which sucks out my oxygen, stealing another breath. Lord bring me out of this mummy case-like room with no way out. "No Exit- Do Not Enter." Then why has my strength found the way out? Maybe I should watch when it leaks out again. There it goes out of my bones!

"A joyful heart is good medicine,
But a broken spirit dries up the bones." Proverbs 17:22

Is it possible these bones can rise again, in strength? Can they dance and find a way out of the mummy case and breathe fresh life again?

"Then you will see this, and your heart will be
glad, and your bones will flourish like the
new grass." Isaiah 66:14a

Someone please prophesy over these bones which dry and die.

Hopeless Fog

A murky mist clings to my discouraged spirit like a cold, wet blanket as I stumble through a familiar path on this vaporous night. The clouds move in, around, and through me, as if I were fighting for a breathing space.

An ever-present hopelessness anoints my eyes so I can no longer see through such distortion. My cheeks know not which dampness belongs to them or to the cloud of fog which surrounds.

My spirit is the heaviest thing I've ever lifted. Holding up my heavy heart is not like lifting a set of weights where I am rewarded with bigger muscles, just the ache.

I'm done carrying it around with no reward attached. Where do I go to discard my weighty spirit and how do I let it go? My fingerprints are deeply engraved on this "weight of hopelessness" as I have gripped it for so long.

The fog is diminishing and withdrawing from the night. From so long ago, I remember the sun and my face hopes for a new day.

"Therefore, since we have so great a cloud of witnesses surrounding us, let us also lay aside every encumbrance and the sin which so easily entangles us, and let us run with endurance the race that is set before us," Hebrews 12:1

Scatter the Night

Solitary and desolate sounds pour forth from beneath the covers announcing the unsolicited presence of dawn. Shoulders soon sag again into an already moist pillow, tossed and smashed from a night's battle.

The blanket doesn't change what lies beneath.
It just covers up the begging for a postponement of the day's beginning by stumbling over yesterday's belongings and last night's cup of misery, now cold and diminished.

He knows the darkness of my night as it grows thin. The shaft of His first light now mixes with my indigo cavern of enclosing walls of insanity. Twisted sheets betray the undoing of a solitary soul against the Prince of darkness.

Blinding Light! You have been here before and brought strength even to that dawn. I lean on the memory of those mornings and His presence soon scatters the broken pieces of my night. The Son will come again.

Trash Bag

A trash bag blows around the parking lot. The wind is in control, not the bag, which is crumpled, dirty, and no longer useful. When the wind lifts it, I wonder if it feels exhilarated and if all is well? The wind slams it into the ground and immediately into the cars. It finds momentary release under a truck, as if hiding, hoping to not be seen.

If I am just quiet, he won't find me. I'm dirty and useless, blown around, slammed into the ground. Strutting around, muscles taut and a jerking head oozes disgust out of his mouth "You are fat, ugly, and stupid."

Jesus picks up the trash bag, cleans it off and says, "You are mine, not his." Was it me hiding under the truck or was it me in that old Volkswagen? I was in the closet curled up in a ball. Jesus says, "I won't hurt you, because I love you. You are beautiful. I bought you for an ever greater price. Now pour out My love for you to others and wash them in the Word."

Black Canyon of the Gunnison River
Ode to the Death of a Marriage

The river continues to cut through layers of rock on its descent. Now jagged canyon walls and boulders reveal evidence of a Precambrian span 2700 feet down.

I watched him scrambling deeper into the narrow canyon on that treacherous quest. It was not unlike his earlier swift trips into anger and his plunges into rivers of rage. They cut with vengeance and took us into the deepening journey of the black canyon of our marriage.

I remained above on the rim of the canyon and noticed the power of that river. I grieved the widening distance while watching him get smaller and farther from me as he reached the bottom. I choose instead to crawl into a cave within the caverns of my mind.

Many would say it took "billions and billions" of years for the river to make the canyon. It only took us 33 years.

Winds of Winter

I descended beneath layers of snow and ice where degrees also drop and easily freeze fingers, which try to dig through hard, wintry barriers. There you'll find tiny, tender roots waiting patiently for their cue to a grand entrance.

Spring lies like a leopard waiting to pounce forth with all its energy of new life. Those tiny white roots explode up into a green spear like a sword slicing through that last layer of snow. The crocus is only encouraged by a harsh winter, bursting into bloom with striking color.

I find myself in a wintry spirit, and my soul is immobilized into slushy stillness. I don't want to dig through the frozen tundra even to possibly find tender roots. I just want to stay in the place of absolute zero activity, where I feel secure. Yet even here, lies a tender root preserved in the Holiest place of my being, protected from the biting winds of legalism disguised as love. The rays of Grace pour forth onto man's sharp shards of judgment. The Son of Righteousness begins to shine on nearly frozen roots and awakens them to His promise of the return of spring and His final return.

"My beloved responded and said to me, Arise my darling, my beautiful one, and come along. For behold, the winter is past. The rain is over and gone." Song of Solomon 2:10-11

My Mind Just Ran Out of Ink

I can hear my thoughts that no longer ring true with neither precision nor boldness. They just seem disorderly and do not pierce the space of my day, or am I still fighting with the night?

My spirit in this darkness, slowly sinks down within the clutter of my mind. Tears do not even flow upon this dry and cracked face where others have traveled for nearly a century.

Tender, new memories even seem marred and silent. They barely utter a distorted whisper into my cobwebbed brain as they submerge somewhere into a realm of dormancy, nowhere to be found ever again

My silver pen no longer sparkles and its ink seems dried-up. Words that previously flowed forth now wander aimlessly around, and they barely find a place on this paper.

Pebble of Truth

Running towards the battle line of my monstrous Goliath, I notice that he fights with fear and intimidation. He expects me to quiver at the sound of his heavy armor, contemptuously lumbering forward as he shouts lies about my lack of strength.

David's words thundered out at the approaching taunts, hidden within Goliath's impenetrable armor:
"This day the LORD will deliver you into my hands and I will strike you down and remove your head from you." I Samuel 17:46

I pick up a stone of truth from within my spiritual armor and hold it firmly. Its smoothness fits well in my grip as I hurl it into my Goliath and deliver a frontal lobotomy.

I must still cut off any ties that I have to this fallen giant and disconnect the head of that furnace of fear from its now useless body.

News Flash: One speedy little mouse protected by the armor of God knocked down a quarter-ton giant with a pebble of tumbled and weathered truth. Some thought it might have been an elephant hiding in plain sight.

Chapter 6

Lift Up Your Eyes

"I lift up my eyes to the hills. Where does my help come from? My help comes from the LORD, the maker of heavens and earth." Psalms 121:1-2 NIV

Many times in scripture (over 60) we are reminded to, "lift up our eyes" and see or listen and hear Him. When I have been down in spirit, my eyes were looking at the problem: the pain, the mess, and not at Him. Look up and see Him where our help is. Then, let your spirit follow your eyes. He will tell you what is next as, "My sheep hear My voice".

Even when Abraham was about to sacrifice Isaac, (Genesis 22:13 NASV) "he raised his eyes and looked and behold, behind him a ram was caught in the thicket by his thorns."

"Isaac went out to meditate on his journey to find his bride. He lifted up his eyes and looked. And he saw her coming on a camel." Genesis 24:63b

"Rebekah lifted up her eyes and saw Isaac." Genesis 24:64

The last few years of my counseling career were really not my counseling as such. It became much more a "Listening Prayer" as noted in the book by Leanne Payne who has passed on and left many of her writings. I consider her style to be one of lifting up your eyes and ears and listening to the LORD for the client. The Holy Spirit is then the counselor who knows a whole lot more about them than I do. It was my greatest hope for them that they would end up being able to hear or know the LORD's desire for themselves.

Fill your life up with Jesus.

Fly Into His Arms

Ride down the banister of life. It isn't just hope; it is faith Yeshua will catch me as He sent me on this journey. He sings over me with joy as I fly into His arms.

Today's Container of Time

Every minute before this has been preparation for stepping into a new one, or a celebration for leaving the previous moment. Today is yesterday's tomorrow, soon to become a new yesterday.

The sun I saw this morning creeping up was spawning a new dawn. How can that ancient ball bring forth a brand new container of time every 24 hours? It is for such a time as this; it's a second chance, a new beginning, a finishing touch, a new birth, a celebration, an end or a conclusion. It's that first step, next step, or last step.

Whether this 24 hour container of time is viewed as a crystal vase or a beat up tin cup, it is a holder of time. We generally choose what goes into it, but we cannot change the container size; 1440 minutes is all we get. How we use it, however, is foundation for the rest we are given.

Fill each container to the top. Leave no empty space. Fill it with works glorifying God.

Worm Trading

Dedicated to My Grandson, Daniel
By Gram Gram

Worms of apparent hopelessness lie in the bottom of a rusty can. They are waiting for the young fisherman to try one more time to catch his prize of the day that lies in the depths of murky waters.

The can of squishy, fat worms is traded for his fullness of manhood. Then that whiskery old fish took a chance and grabbed onto a piece of wiggling life, looking like a tasty snack.

A young man now hauls in his prize; he grabs the empty can of hopelessness and continues his walk into his future of hope and adulthood.

Wonders Yet to Be

A shimmering lunar likeness floats in a dark night pond, then breaks apart as a fallen leaf slides into the obscurity of a prophetic wonder.

I look up to see what sent the crumpled leaf down to become as a floating barge announcing the death of a king. From Your heavens, I see a manuscript of what is to come. Each flicker in the sky, named by You, is but a note on Your page. It shouts to me of the wonders yet to be.

I yearn to know what they say. You taught the Prophet Daniel long ago to speak of the stars to his wise men so they might recognize Your coming.

Show me now the wonders yet to be.

Entrance Into Eternity

Shofar* sounds break through the heavenlies as another saint approaches.

All is well. Come quickly as the temple trembles and the torn curtain parts. Thunder rumbles and shakes the lampstand. Another saint now dances on the doorstep of the Holy of Holies dancing before her King.

All is well. Come quickly YHWH*. Soon she will run through the lilies of the valley.

He waits. Her Rose of Sharon loves her. He died for her. He waits. He rose for her. He waits.

All is well. Come quickly, my Messiah*.

The shofar proclaims a life well lived, and it announces arrivals into the city. Her feet are reflected on the streets and now over the sea of glass.

All is well.

*shofar: a ram's horn, used by the Israelites to summon the people to battle or to gather for worship
*YHWH: Hebrew name of God and is pronounced "Yahweh" or "Jehovah"
*Messiah: the anointed one

Chapter 7

Jesus our Messiah

In 2001, prior to 9/11, two groups of Christians from Fort Collins, Colorado crossed the United States from East to West and North to South while praying for the nation. One group drove from San Francisco to Washington, D.C. The other group, which I was in, made the cross complete by praying from Canada to Mexico through North Dakota and straight down into Texas and the Gulf.

Both teams celebrated communion at the borders of our country and at the crossing point of both journeys. The cross piece is where I believe Christs' head would have been during his crucifixion.

The two poems which follow: Holy War and Spirit Lake were written about the northern journey and occurred near the previously identified "Center of North America".

The entire chapter embraces Jesus as the only way for one hurting, depressed, lost person, or lost nation, to find a glorious way up.

Spirit Lake

A mighty Sioux war party returned from a forbidden night battle across "Minnewaukan Seche". The Great Spirit drowned the warriors and to this day; Satan keeps it for himself: Lake of the Evil Spirit.

Waves slash against the rocks beneath our feet. Ravens and blackbirds watch us in fly-by attacks because of our threatening presence. These enemy spies warn of another Spirit's presence.

This northern lake was rededicated by a band of warriors of the Holy Spirit. It was renamed, "Lake of the Holy Spirit", to The Greater Spirit.

Holy War

A prophetic wonder shaped like a giant black eagle appears in the darkening sky. It moves into a position of declaration, and the cloud announces that the battle has begun. Lightning, beyond earthly understanding, bursts from East to West, cracking and breaking apart the once black night. Our earthly forms are shaking from thunderous sounds which assault our ears. Angels, whose battle is displayed before our dimensionally limited eyes, contend for power over the geographical center of North America.

The army of Yeshua gallops into battle to the gates of Hell. We are dressed for Victory and clothed in Glory; nothing penetrates our shields of salvation. Swords are drawn and drip with Words of The Most High. Faith hurls any arrows of attack back into the Spiritual forces of darkness, and it thunders into the wind.

"Then the earth shook and quaked; and the foundations of the mountains were trembling and were shaken because He was angry." Psalms 18:7

"He sent out His arrows, and scattered them and lighting flashes in abundance, and routed them". Psalms 18:14

Holy is the LORD.

White Linen of Sinlessness

The tabernacle stood arrayed in twined flaxen linen. It was set apart in the wilderness for the LORD to come and meet with them. It was as if a tallit* was surrounding His glory in this temporary place in the desert.

"For in the day of trouble, He will conceal me in His tent. He will hide me. He will lift me up on a rock." Psalms 27: 5

Even His body was covered with white linen before He descended below instead of me.

It will cover His heavenly army dressed "in fine linen, white and clean." Revelation 19:14

The tabernacle was draped in linen and wrapped as a bride.

"Let us rejoice and be glad and give the glory to Him, for the marriage of the Lamb has come and His bride has made herself ready." Revelation 19:7 NASV

He gave her fine, white linen in which to clothe herself.

"Come My Bride. Come to the marriage supper of the Lamb." Revelation 19:9

*tallit: Jewish prayer shawl

Escaping an Active Volcano

Oh no! I'm standing on the edge of a volcano. Why didn't someone tell me I was getting so dangerously close?

"Well it makes a lot of noise and it gets hotter and hotter the closer you get to it and it vomits up red hot stones."

That's the way he was: making lots of noise, yelling and screaming, stomping around and throwing words that hit my stomach and burned my heart.

It was time to step away from the pit because one never knew when it would erupt. Some are drawn to danger or believe the myth, "maybe it won't explode anymore."

How does one step away when the Volcano is already erupting? Ropes representing safety have burned through and the ground is igniting your shoes. It's either turn and run or be transformed into a melted mess of nothingness. It's like the Black Hole death of a collapsing star when gravity squashes it into nothingness.

Missing Pieces

The last puzzle is nearly complete. Its border was long ago defined and most of the pieces are on the table. God declares their final destination; yet I hear scholars telling me where He is going to put the next piece as they brilliantly declare the end of age.

"That piece will go over here." Equally magnificent minds defiantly proclaim, with certainty. "No, there is no way. It has to go there." One of them grabs at a piece of theology and tries to force it into place. "Look, if you just shave a little bit off, it will fit perfectly."

Shredding pieces of God's prophetic Word to make them fit into end time paradigms is just as distasteful as arguing over where and when they will be out in place. Yet, to God, it is sacrilegious to deface His Word.

Chapter 8

Peace and The Exchanged Life

The parable that Jesus told in Matthew 25:1-13, about the ten virgins, speaks to me of the five who had not put oil in their lamps were not ready to receive Christ's return. Was this possibly referring to receiving the Holy Spirit? They were turned away from the door to the wedding of the bridegroom, Jesus. He said, "I tell you the truth, I don't know you."

When we have exchanged our sin-filled life and received eternal life by His death and resurrection, we have oil in our lamps and will hear, "Welcome Wise Virgin."

"When you were dead in your transgressions and the uncircumcision of your flesh, He made you alive together with Him, having forgiven us all our transgressions." Colossians 2:13

Mother Teresa is an example of one who had a truly exchanged life.

"For to me, to live is Christ and to die is gain." Philippians 1:21

"I have been crucified with Christ and it is no longer I who live but Christ who lives in me." Galatians 2:20

An Exchanged Life

The Voice echoes from the cave, "Come in. See what lies before you." Wrappings and bindings betray what has been passively entombed and consequently disguises the life within as dead.

Bindings bend and separate the strips of man-made wrappings designed to imprison and deceive the outside world of what has lain lifeless far too long. He now comes forth as one birthed into new life.

The unwrapped man now stands at the cave's entrance, waiting to step out as his earthly Abba comes in and lies down. The bindings now go back into familiar folds and holding places as they cover the truly dead.

"Come forth, oh man of God. Come forth."

Mountain Stream of Consciousness

Sounds slice through and begin another baptism of my soul. Mountain water cleanses my mind and washes off the dust of grinding responsibilities. Cold sprays of water remind me of a thirst for God.

Shoulders made to sit up straight and hold other people's worries, troubles, and griefs can now slope in ease.

The alliteration of sounds seem to usher in a tranquility that soothes the ache in my soul as burdens can now slide off into His stream of love.

Further downstream, away from the source of pain, the sound quiets and the stream begins to caress my mind with a Rocky Mountain memory.

The LORD's Lullaby

Drips
Dripping
Into my heart as Thy words press into my cheek and sleep rolls down my eyelids. Energy leaks out into my dreams where I run in fields forever with the Holy Spirit blowing through my hair.

Drips
Dripping
Silence slides in and stillness quenches my thirst for peace as I am lulled by the softness of His rain drip dance, His lullaby slows. Sweet peace has thoroughly anointed my soul, and placed words of peace into my heart.

Drip
Drip

The Lord's lullaby is accompanied by the rain washing off my deck and a soft resonance falling from my roof. Drops slow into silence, sending my soul to sleep.

"My beloved responded and said to me, Arise my darling, my beautiful one, and come along. For behold, the winter is past."
Song of Solomon 2:10-11

Metamorphosis

What protection covers me when I'm lost in a desert of despair without a chrysalis in the making? What covering comes between me and a sand storm barrage on my temple and spirit where God tabernacles with me?

"Let me dwell in Your tent forever. Let me take refuge in the shelter of Your wings." Psalms 61:4

The butterfly's protection before its metamorphic change was a cocoon covering its squishy body. This simple case covered and kept this amazing insect from the dangerous world.

"Do you not know that you are a temple of God and that the Spirit of God dwells in you?" I Corinthians 3:16

It's the new covenant covering that surrounds and protects me. It is similar to the other desert covering where the tabernacle stood while waiting for the now perfect covenant. It was surrounded by twined, flaxen linen covering the presence of a Holy God amidst His people.

"Let them conduct a sanctuary for Me, that I may dwell among them." Exodus 25:8

"As You clothed man in the beginning in skin, You will clothe us in white robes at the beginning of our eternal life with You. Yet now I offer my body as a living sacrifice as an act of worship."
Romans 12:1

When I was naked, you clothed me, surely now You will clothe me in a monarch's beauty as I break out of this cocoon.

"For in the day of trouble He will conceal me in His tabernacle; in the secret place of His tent, He will hide me; He will lift me up on a rock." Psalms 27:5

Feet

"I am thirsty. Have you anything to drink?"

An old withered street lady, enveloped by the aroma of someone else's discarded lunch from days ago, walks a familiar path down the back alley beside her shopping cart. Who has ever held her grimy, wrinkled hands, or embraced her rumpled life? Were there babies she once held and caressed or ever nursed?

Life has become a tsunami over her and ripped out any previous spark in her eyes which now only seek out a vision of the ground, having given up on looking up.

She sees the feet of another standing before her own increasing exhaustion. "May I give you water? I don't want you to thirst."

She thirsts. She drinks and leaves the presence of those feet, having been unwilling to lift up her eyes and gaze upon the one who noticed. She returns to her small corner of life to share the water with another. "His feet are so beautiful. Please drink His water."

"If any man is thirsty, let him come to Me and drink." John 7:37

He Rides the Wings of the Wind

"He lays the beams of His upper chambers on their waters; He makes the clouds His chariots; He rides on the wings of the wind;" Psalms 104:3

Oh the wonders of Your path under the chambers of heavenly showers. Breathe on me as we walk; remind my face of who created the wind. Oh Lord, my God, the heavens stretch out before us, and soon you must roll them up like a curtain on this crumbling stage.

Fragrance of Christ

A sinful woman stood behind Christ at a Pharisee's house. Weeping at his dusty feet, she washed them with her tears and dried them with her hair, "kissed them and poured perfume on them,"
Luke 7:36-38

The woman, probably uninvited, came to see Christ with an expensive jar of perfume. She knew she was a sinner and that Jesus had something even more precious for her.

Can you imagine how she might never want to wash her hands or hair again after drying his feet with her own hair and with her hands anointing the feet that would soon have holes in them?

May the fragrance of Christ stay with you forever.

Worship Notes

My silver pen becomes an instrument of worship. It is poised above a silent, cold, white piece of paper and explodes into a crescendo as it spreads ink across meaningful places. It's like a conductor's baton, creating loops, swirls, jots, and tittles, bringing meaning onto this staff of worship.

Ink began to be absorbed by papyrus even as His blood dripped down into that thirsty dust within the shadow of the cross. Whether it is a silver pen or an animal's quill, worship will happen. Even the rocks will join in praise.

Words are carefully placed to coax others out of their routine ways of thinking. Sentences become a treasure box of luscious notes all meant to be together one after the other. What was once plain and lifeless now powerfully portrays a new way to look at life and praise its creator. May these word notes roll off a tongue and feel different in the mouth as they elicit new thoughts and join the angels in worship.

Printed in the United States
By Bookmasters